Contemplation

Introduction

All perfect praise is due to Allaah Who rose above the worlds in rank and essence ; He overwhelmed His creation with His glory, might and power and commanded us to contemplate His verses and creation with our hearts and minds. His might and exaltedness confounds the hearts of those seeking His pleasure.

Whenever they think they have reached the answer in their quest to know about Him, His endless astonishing might makes them give up and stop attempting to find the limit and boundaries of His might and glory.

And when they attempt to give up, they are called to persevere in their search and ponder upon His attributes through the eye of servitude; they are called to contemplate upon their own creation to realize the extent and magnitude of His bounties, and to express gratitude for every bounty and glorify Him for every one and for the number of times these bounties are renewed. They are called to reflect on His Decrees and how they result in distinguishing people between believers and disbelievers, losers and winners, good people and evil people, and the appreciative and ungrateful.May Allaah exalt the mention of Prophet Muhammad, sallallaahu 'alayhi wa sallam, the master of the children of Aadam, who did not consider his lofty status something to brag or boast about, and may Allaah exalt the mention of his household and his Companions who became shining stars.

To proceed : **Contemplation is one of the great actions of the heart; in fact, it is the absolute best deed. 'Umar ibn 'Abdul-'Azeez, may Allaah have mercy on him, said:"Contemplating on the bounties of Allaah is the best act of worship."** [1]

Contemplation is the key to the light of guidance, the starting point of certitude and the source of knowledge and understanding. A wise scholar once said: "Make your heart live by admonishments and enlighten it through contemplation." [2]

Many people know the virtue of contemplation but are unaware of its reality and fruits. However, few are those who actually contemplate. Allaah Says (what means): *"And how many a sign within the heavens and earth do they pass over while they, there from, are turning away. And most of them believe not in Allaah except while they associate others with Him."* [QUR'AAN 12:105-106]

The best gatherings are those in which people contemplate on the Names and Attributes of Allaah, His Paradise and Hell, His reward and punishment, His favors and signs which He mentioned in His Book and can be observed in the universe, and His creation. The one who is blessed to attend such gatherings will surely taste its sweetness and goodness.

1 Hilyat Al-Awliyaa' (314/5).
2 Tafseer Ibn Katheer (305/3).

What is the definition of contemplation?
What is the ruling of contemplation?
What are the fields and areas one should contemplate on?
What are the fruits and benefits of contemplation?
How were our Salaf with regards to this great act of worship?

The definition of contemplation

Linguistically: **It means to think, reflect, and observe. It is extracted from the word Fikr. It also refers to the heart thinking again and again about something with the intention of extracting lessons admonishments.**

Terminologically: **It is when the heart searches for implications of what it observes. It was also said that it refers to the heart searching for the meaning or essence of things.**
At-Taahir ibn 'Aashoor, may Allaah have mercy on him, said: "Contemplating is when the heart looks to benefit from sound knowledge."[1]

[1] At-Tahreer Wat-Tanweer (Page 1299).

The ruling of contemplation

Many evidences prove that contemplating is an obligation upon the believers, whether it is upon the Qur'aanic verses, the creation of Allaah, one's own creation, the punishment of Allaah, the fire of Hell, or upon the reward of Allaah and His Paradise. Allaah Says (what means):

"And We Sent not before you except men to whom We revealed [Our message] so ask the people of the message [i.e. former scriptures] if you do not know. [We sent them] with clear proofs and written ordinances. And We revealed to you the message [i.e. the Qur'aan] that you may make clear to the people what was sent down to them and that they might contemplate." [QUR'AAN 16:43-44]

The verses show that the revelation of the Qur'aan was intended for nothing else except so that people would contemplate on it. Allaah The Almighty praised in His Book His slaves who contemplate, Saying (what means):

"Indeed, in the creation of the heavens and the earth and the alteration of the night and the day are signs for those of understanding. Who remember Allaah while standing or sitting or [lying] on their sides and contemplate on the creation of the heavens and the earth, [saying]: 'Our Lord, You did not create this aimlessly; exalted are You [above such a thing]; then protect us from the punishment of the Fire. Our Lord, indeed whoever You admit to the Fire-You

have disgraced him, and for the wrongdoers there are no helpers." [QUR'AAN 3:190-192]

'Ataa`, may Allaah have mercy on him, said:

"Once, 'Ubayd ibn 'Umayr and I visited 'Aa`ishah, may Allaah be pleased with her. 'Ubayd ibn 'Umayr said to her: 'Tell us the most extraordinary experience of the Messenger of Allaah, sallallaahu 'alayhi wa sallam.' She kept silent for a while, wept and said: 'Everything about him was extraordinary. One night, he said: 'Let me worship my Lord.' I said to him: 'By Allaah, I enjoy your closeness and I like to see you worshipping your Lord.' He, sallallaahu 'alayhi wa sallam, got up, performed ablution without using a lot of water. Then, he started praying and cried until he wet his beard. He prostrated in Sujood and cried until he wet the floor. Then, he lay down on his side and cried. When the time of the Fajr Prayer came, Bilaal came to announce it and said to the Prophet, sallallaahu 'alayhi wa sallam: 'Why are you crying while Allaah has forgiven your first and last sins?' The Prophet, sallallaahu 'alayhi wa sallam, replied: *'Allaah has revealed tonight the following verse* **(which means):** *"Verily in the creation of the heavens and the earth, and the alteration of the night and day, there are indeed signs for men of understanding..."*

He, sallallaahu 'alayhi wa sallam, added: *"Woe unto the one who recites it without thinking deeply about it."* [1]

This narration proves that the one who does not contemplate on these verses is threatened with punishment, and Allaah does not threaten to punish for something unless it opposes His command, which means that contemplating is an obligatory matter.

Allaah The Almighty mentioned contemplation in the Qur'aan coupled with signs and examples, and commanded His slaves to contemplate over these examples. Allaah The Almighty Says (what means): *"Would one of you like to have a garden of palm trees and grapevines underneath which rivers flow in which he has from every fruit? But he is afflicted with old age and has weak [i.e. immature] offspring, and it is hit by a whirlwind containing fire and is burned. Thus does Allaah make clear to you [His] verses that you might contemplate."* [QUR'AAN 2:266]

This man's heart was attached to the garden for different reasons:

- **It was a large garden and not a small farm.**
- **It had different types of trees in addition to palm trees and grapevines.**

1 Reported by Ibn Hibbaan (620) and Al-Albaani ruled it as authentic.

- The water in the garden was not fetched from a well, rather it come from rivers that ran through the garden and no effort was exerted in getting it.
- He had become old and people usually like to have a source of income when they reach old age.
- He had young and ill children, and they had no source of income except this garden.

Since the level of attachment to this garden was very high, what kind of disappointment and grief would he feel if his garden was hit by a whirlwind and burned?

Allaah The Almighty concluded the verse Saying (what means): **"Thus does Allaah make clear to you [His] verses that you might contemplate."** Meaning that He, The Almighty, gave this example so that His slaves contemplate and give this example thought.

When one contemplates over this verse and gives it thought, as Allaah wanted us to do, one discovers that this example is meant to resemble the owner of this garden with that of a person who gives charity and keeps boasting about it and reminding the person to whom he gave it. On the Day of Resurrection, when a person needs every single reward he earned to make his scale of good deeds heavy this person will discover that his deeds will be like dust dispersed. The situation of the owner of the garden when his garden is burnt will be like that of the person who destroyed his reward of spending charity because of boasting about it and reminding those to whom he

gave it. Contemplating about this example and this resemblance leads the person to realize the importance of sincerity when performing good deeds.

In another example, Allaah The Almighty Says (what means): *"The example of [this] worldly life is but like rain which We have sent down from the sky that the plants of the earth absorb, [those] from which men and livestock eat, until, when the earth has taken on its adornment and is beautified and its people suppose that they have capability over it, there comes to it Our command by night or by day, and We make it as a harvest [its vegetation having been utterly destroyed], as if it had not flourished yesterday. Thus do We explain in detail the signs for a people who contemplate."* [QUR'AAN 10:24] **This resemblance exposes the reality of this worldly life, and that it is just like the earth that produces the best fruits, and then is afflicted with a disaster which makes it ruined and destroyed, as if it was never full of fruits or vegetables in it before.**

Allaah The Almighty Says (what means): *"Not equal are the companions of the Fire and the companions of Paradise. The companions of Paradise, they are the attainers [of success]. If We had sent down this Quran upon a mountain, you would have seen it humbled and coming apart from fear of Allaah. And these examples We present to the people that perhaps they will contemplate."* [QUR'AAN 59:20-21] **Man should**

contemplate over this Qur'aan and its powerful impact; Allaah is telling us that if it were sent down on a mountain, it would demolish it, then how should its impact be on our hearts?

Allaah The Exalted enumerated for His slaves the variety of His creation in the Heavens and the earth and the different bounties and blessings He bestowed upon them in order that they contemplate.

Allaah The Almighty Says (what means):

- *"It is Allaah who erected the heavens without pillars that you [can] see; then He established Himself above the Throne and made subject [for the benefit of mankind] the sun and the moon, each running [course] for a specified term. He arranges [each] matter; He details the signs that you may, of the meeting with your Lord, be certain. And it is He who spread the earth and placed therein firmly set mountains arid rivers; and from all of the fruits He made therein two mates; He causes the night to cover the day. Indeed in that are signs for a people who contemplate."* [QUR'AAN 13:2-3]
- *"It is He who sends down rain from the sky; from it is drink and from it is foliage in which you pasture [animals]. He causes to grow for you thereby the crops, olives, palm trees, grape vines, and from all the*

fruits. Indeed in that is a sign for a people who contemplate. And He has subjected for you the night and day and the sun and moon, and the stars are subjected by His command. Indeed in that are signs for a people who reason. And [He has subjected] whatever He multiplied for you on the earth of varying colors. Indeed in that is a sign for a people who remember. And it is He who subjected the sea for you to eat from it tender meat and to extract from it ornaments which you wear. And you see the ships plowing through it, and [He subjected it] that you may seek of His bounty; and perhaps you will be grateful."
[Qur'aan 16:10-14]

People are commanded to contemplate on the final outcome of the nations before them and why they were destroyed: were they weak people who could not stand the punishment that befell them, or were they powerful and strong nations but could not stand in the face of the soldiers of Allaah? Allaah The Almighty Says (what means): *"Do they not contemplate concerning themselves? Allaah has not created the heavens and the earth and what is between them except in truth and for a specified term. And indeed, many of the people, in [the matter of] the meeting with their Lord, are disbelievers. Have they not traveled through the earth and observed how the end of those before them was? They were greater than* *them in power, and they plowed [or excavated] the earth and built it up more than they [i.e. the Makkans] have built it up, and their messengers came to them with clear evidences. And Allaah would not ever have wronged them, but they were wronging themselves."* **[QUR'AAN 30:8-9]**

Our Salaf, may Allaah have mercy on them, were aware and heedful of the obligation of contemplation and thus used to command their students to contemplate. Abu Sulaymaan Ad-Daaraani, may Allaah have mercy on him, used to say : "Get your eyes used to crying and your heart to contemplating."[1]

---

1 Hilyat Al-Awliyaa' (274/9).

Types of contemplation and its fields

Contemplation has boundaries which a Muslim must know and stay within, and not allow himself to go beyond these limits. For example, a Muslim should not contemplate on the essence of Allaah The Almighty or how His attributes are or how He does certain things.

Ibn 'Umar, may Allaah be pleased with him, said: "Contemplate over the favors and signs of Allaah but not the essence of Allaah The Almighty." [1]

Ibn 'Abbaas, may Allaah be pleased with him, said: "Contemplate over everything except the essence of Allaah." [2]

If the slave finds himself contemplating over something like this (i.e. the essence of Allaah and His attributes) he should immediately stop and seek refuge in Allaah from such thoughts, and start thinking of other things.

One may contemplate over things that are useless both in this worldly life as well as the Hereafter, like someone contemplating over how a certain sportsperson performs in the game and how he does what he does during the game. Some

---

1 I'tiqaad Ahl As-Sunnah (525/3) and Al-Albaani ruled it as sound (Hasan).

2 Reported by Ibn Battah in his book Al-Inaabah (108) and Ibn Hajar ruled it as good in his book Fat-h Al-Baari (383/13) .

people may contemplate over the way a singer rehearses or how one of his favorite actors acts in his movies. Things could even reach to forbidden contemplation, like if someone starts to contemplate the beauty of a woman. All these are examples of dispraised contemplation that are of no benefit for the slave in this worldly life and in the Hereafter.

Praiseworthy contemplation is that which makes the slave achieve the sought fruits and benefits of contemplation. Ibn Al-Qayyim, may Allaah have mercy on him, said: "An important rule is that evil and virtue result from contemplation, because contemplation is the origin of will and determination in everything, asceticism, refraining from doing something, loving something or hating something. The most beneficial types of contemplation are contemplation over the following:

- Things that would result in a benefit for the Hereafter
- The way to attain such benefits
- How to protect oneself against matters that harm in the Hereafter
- The way to avoid such harmful matters
- Things that would result in a benefit for this worldly life
- The way to attain such benefits
- How to protect oneself against matters that harm in this worldly life
- The way to avoid such harmful matters

These eight categories are the types which sound-minded people contemplate over. The most important type in the first category is contemplating over the signs and favors of Allaah, His prohibitions and commands, and how to learn about Allaah, His Names and Attributes, His Book (the Qur'aan), the Sunnah of His Prophet, sallallaahu 'alayhi wa sallam, and things leading to this knowledge." [1]

What are the fields and areas which a slave should contemplate over in order to benefit and attain some fruits? What are the things which a slave should contemplate over in order to get a beneficial result and win (in both lives)?

Contemplating over one's own self :

Allaah The Almighty commanded us to contemplate about our own selves, and dispraised the polytheists Saying (what means): *"Do they not contemplate concerning themselves."* [QUR'AAN 30:8] Contemplating over one's own self is worthier than contemplating over other creation, because it is closer to the person than anything else, and one knows his conditions and situations more than anything else.

If one contemplates over his creation he will discover the greatness of his Creator and the signs of magnificence of Allaah within his own creation; the one who knows his creation will know the greatness of his Lord.

Contemplating over one's own self includes the following:

1 Al-Fawaa'id (pg. 198).

- **Contemplating over the way Allaah created man, his body, his shape, and instilled his sense of hearing and sight.**
- **Contemplating over one's faults. This is very important because one cannot correct himself if he does not contemplate in order to recognize his faults and areas of weakness. If one contemplates correctly, he will be able to discover his mistakes and faults and work on changing himself and correcting it and refrain from committing them again.**
- **Contemplating over his family, wife and children; Allaah created for us spouses from ourselves, and our children came out from our backs (i.e. the sperms that are instilled in the man's back). We are also part of our fathers and mothers. Therefore, contemplating over these people is part of contemplating over one's own self. One should contemplate over their conditions, deeds, the problems and faults in the family that must be addressed and the best way they can be reformed.**

Contemplating over the creation of the heavens and the earth and the wonders of the universe:

The wonders which Allaah The Almighty instilled in His creation reflect His greatness and might and astonish those who contemplate over them.

Why should people contemplate over the creation of the heavens and the earth and the wonders of the universe?

Abdur-Rahmaan As-Si'di, may Allaah have mercy on him, answers this question saying: "People should people contemplate over the creation of the heavens and the earth and the wonders of the universe in order to reach the intended objective behind its creation. This proves that contemplation is an act of worship which devout knowledgeable worshippers perform and are known for it. When they contemplate over these things, they realize that Allaah did not create them purposelessly, and thus the response would be, as Allaah informs us Saying (what means): *"Our Lord, You did not create this aimlessly; exalted are You [above such a thing]."* [QUR'AAN 3:191] **Exalted are You our Lord above anything that is not befitting to Your Glory and Magnificence."** [1]

One should utilize experimental and natural sciences and benefit from them in his contemplation. There are many aspects of creation which people know of now, and which our Salaf were never exposed to and never knew of during their time; Allaah The Exalted Says (what means): *"And He creates that which you do not know."* [QUR'AAN 16:8]

Allaah The Exalted creates things which we do not know in the deepest parts of oceans, in caves and in the skies; Allaah The

1 Tayseer Al-Kareem Ar-Rahmaan (161).

Exalted Says (what means): *"Exalted is He who created all pairs [all species] from what the earth grows and from themselves and from that which they do not know."* [QUR'AAN 36:36]

Contemplating over the favors of Allaah:

This is one of the important fields of contemplation for the Muslim. One should contemplate over the job Allaah blessed him with, his wife whom Allaah guided to when he never knew her before, the favor of living safely and securely while he hears of bombing incidents and killing that takes place around him in other places.

Contemplating over this worldly life and the Hereafter :

Allaah The Exalted Says (what means): *"Thus Allaah makes clear to you the verses [of revelation] that you might contemplate. [Over] this world and the Hereafter."* [QUR'AAN 2:219-220] **Commenting on this verse, Ibn 'Abbaas, may Allaah be pleased with him, said: "Contemplate over the demise of this worldly life and the approach of the Hereafter and its eternity."** [1]

Qataadah, may Allaah have mercy on him, said: "Perhaps that you would contemplate over this worldly life and the Hereafter

1 Tafseer At-Tabari (369/2).

and thus realize the virtue of the Hereafter over this worldly life." [1]

Things that are prohibited when contemplating

Allaah The Exalted Says (what means): *"And produce you in that [form] which you do not know."* [QUR'AAN 56:61] **This verse proves that there are things concerning the creation of humankind which are hidden from them and it is not possible to know it, and thus one is not permitted to contemplate over them.**

This is what differentiates between Muslims and non-Muslims in the way they look at things and evaluate them. The atheistic way of weighing and judging things believes that one can find out anything and everything through experience, while the Islamic way of weighing and judging things admits that there are limits which one should not go beyond.

For example, had the disbelievers known that Allaah kept the knowledge of certain things to Himself, they would not have wasted a lot of time on experiments trying to discover the essence of the human soul. They would have stopped these experiments which consume a great portion of resources, and made many people have doubts and misconceptions regarding

1 Tafseer At-Tabari (369/2).

creed and faith. Allaah The Exalted Says (what means): *"And they ask you, [O Muhammad] about the soul. Say: 'The soul is of the affair [i.e. concern] of my Lord. And you [i.e. mankind] have not been given of knowledge except a little."* [QUR'AAN 17:85]

In addition to this, there are many other matters of the Unseen whose reality man can never discover, like the angels, Jinn and so on. These are matters which a Muslim should refrain from contemplating over and limit himself to things which Islaam allows and not go beyond them, simply because they are from the Unseen which can never be discovered through experiments or contemplation.

Let us read the following statement of a scholar who contemplated the creation of man, animals, and the heavens and the earth; Al-Ghazaali, may Allaah have mercy on him, said:

> **"One of the signs of Allaah is the creation of humankind, who was created from a drop of sperm. O mankind, the closest thing to you is your own self, and in you are many wonders that reflect the greatness of Allaah The Almighty. It would take ages for a person to discover a very small number of them, and yet you are heedless of these wonders that are instilled in you.**

O you who is heedless of his own self, how can you long to know the essence of other than yourself while you are ignorant of your reality and essence? Allaah commanded you to contemplate over your own self in the Qur'aan Saying (what means): *"And in yourselves. Then will you not see?"* [QUR'AAN 51:21]

Remember that you are created from a filthy drop of sperm, as Allaah The Exalted Says (what means): *"Destroyed [i.e. cursed] is man [who denies Allaah's message]; how disbelieving is he. From what thing [i.e. substance] did He create him? From a sperm-drop He created him and destined for him [provisions, life span, etc.] Then He eased the way for him [in this life]."* [QUR'AAN 17:17-20]

Allaah The Exalted also Says (what means):

- *"And of His signs is that He created you from dust; then, suddenly you were human beings dispersing [throughout the earth]."* [QUR'AAN 30:20]
- *"Had he not been a sperm from semen emitted? Then he was a clinging clot, and [Allaah] created [his form] and proportioned [him]."* [QUR'AAN 75:37-38]

- *"Did We not create you from a liquid disdained? And We placed it in a firm lodging [i.e. the womb]. For a known extent."* [QUR'AAN 77:20-22]
- *"Does man not consider that We created him from a [mere] sperm drop, then at once [as soon as he becomes self-sufficient] he is a clear adversary?"* [QUR'AAN 36:77]
- *"Indeed, We created man from a sperm-drop mixture [of the male and female substance, within the womb] that We may try him; and We made him hearing and seeing."* [QUR'AAN 76:2]

Then Allaah mentions how He changed the sperm drop into a clinging clot, and made the clot into a lump of flesh, and made from the lump, bones. Allaah The Almighty Says (what means): *"And certainly did We create man from an extract of clay. Then We placed him as a sperm drop in a firm lodging [i.e. the womb]."* [QUR'AAN 23:12-13] **Repeating the term 'sperm drop' in the Qur'aan is not meant only so that people hear it mentioned a lot and refrain from contemplating over it.**

If the sperm drop, which is a drop of a filthy liquid, is left in the open and is exposed to air, it would become rotten and stink, but Allaah made it emerge from between the backbone and the ribs.

Look how Allaah joined the male and the female (as spouses) and instilled love and compassion in their hearts.

Look how Allaah led them to unite, driven by their natural desire, love and compassion towards each other.

Look how Allaah extracted the sperm drop from the man as a result of intercourse.

Look how Allaah brought menstrual blood from the woman's veins and collected it in the womb.

Look how Allaah created the fetus from the sperm drop and fed him in the womb until he grew.

Look how Allaah turned the white sperm drop into a red clinging clot and then turned it into a lump of flesh.

Look how Allaah divided the lump of flesh into different parts: bones, nerves, veins, and flesh.

Look how Allaah created man's limbs from this flesh, nerves and veins. He made the head round, and placed in it the eyes, nose, and mouth. He gave man hands and legs and divided the tips of these hands and legs into fingers, and divided the fingers into fingertips.

Look how Allaah after that, created the inner organs, like the heart, the kidney, the lungs, the liver, spleen, lung, uterus, and bladder, and gave each organ a different shape, size and function.

Look how Allaah also divided the organs and limbs into smaller parts, like the eye having seven layers and each layer has a distinct function and shape. If any of the layers or the qualities is lost, the eye would not function.

Look how Allaah made the bone a strong part of the body which originally comes from a thin and weak sperm, but then Allaah created these bones and made them the structure that holds the human body firm. Allaah gave these bones different shapes, sizes and lengths; some are long while others are short, some are hollow and others are solid. Since man needs to move, Allaah did not make all bones one piece, rather many bones connected with joints to facilitate the movement. Allaah shaped each bone according to the body's need during its movements, and connected them with ligaments. Allaah made one end of the bone concave and the end of the place it connects with convex so that they fit perfectly. This enabled the slave to move any part of his body without any problem, and had it not been that Allaah created these joints, movement would not have been possible.

Look how Allaah created the head bones and put them together. These bones are fifty five different bones with

different shapes and fit together to make the final round shape of the head.

Mentioning the number of bones is not intended to count and know the number, but rather to contemplate over the greatness of The One Who created man in this shape and form, and how He gave them these different shapes and sizes. If the number of bones increases by one, then it would be disastrous for humankind, and doctors would have to operate to remove it. Likewise, if the number is less by one bone, then doctors would have to come in and insert a replacement. Doctors look at these numbers in order to operate and know in which direction to go in treatment, while people of contemplation, look at the numbers as a sign of the magnificence and glory of The Creator.

Man also needs to contemplate over the nervous system, veins and arteries: how many of them are there and where do they originate from in the body.

If one contemplates over the human body inside and outside, he would discover amazing things; all of these things were created by Allaah from a drop of sperm. If Allaah created all of these things with these fine details from a single drop, then how would His creation be when it comes to the universe, the heavens, the stars and the galaxies?

What is His wisdom behind their places, shapes, measures, numbers, combining some of them and scattering others, and their different images?

One should not think that an atom's weight from the Kingdom of the heavens is out of the boundaries of His wisdom. As a matter of fact, it was all created with perfection and coherence. It has more wonders than those in the creation of the human body. In fact, the creation of the earth and all that it contains cannot be compared to the creation of the heavens, and this is why Allaah The Exalted Says in the Qur'aan (what means): *"Are you a more difficult creation or is the heaven? He [i.e. Allaah] constructed it."* [QUR'AAN 79:27] **and also (what means):** *"The creation of the heavens and earth is greater than the creation of mankind, but most of the people do not know."* [QUR'AAN 40:57]

Contemplate the drop of sperm and what resulted from it, and then ask yourself this question: if all humans and the Jinn were to collectively attempt to create the sense of sight or hearing, a brain, an ability, a will, knowledge, a soul, bones, veins, skin or hair for this drop, would they be able to create any of them? If they attempt to discover the essence and reality of man's creation after man was created by Allaah, they would still utterly fail.

What is strange about humankind is that if he looks at an image drawn on a wall which was beautifully and precisely drawn to the point that the painter made it very close to the original and actual shape of the person drawn, one would say with amazement: "This looks as if it is a real person!" One would be impressed by the smartness and accuracy of the painter and would be fascinated by him even though the original shape of the human he drew is not his work (creation). Rather it was created by someone else (i.e. Allaah), and all the painter did was to place the paint on the wall in a certain manner to form the final picture.

How would the case be when one contemplates the filthy drop of sperm which came from between the backbone and the ribs of the man, and then Allaah created a human from that and shaped it in the best manner, and divided it into parts, some are similar and others are different (in shape). He created the bones in the best shape and measure, and beautified the inside and the outside of the creation, then organized the veins and nerves and made a path for food to go in from in order for that to be the means for man's existence and survival. Then He turned this drop of sperm into a human and gave him the senses of sight and hearing, and created a backbone for him and made it the foundation and the structure of his body, and instilled in the abdomen the necessary tools to receive food and process it, and placed the senses in the head.

Contemplate what happens to the fetus in the womb: how it was created within three layers of darkness (namely, the belly, the womb, and the amniotic membrane). If one was able to see through and monitor the progress of the fetus and how it grows and develops without any tool to shape it and without anyone touching it; did you ever see a picture coming into existence without a tool or a painter to paint it? Glory be to Allaah, how great is He and how clear are His evidences!

Contemplate: besides the perfect ability of Allaah, He is the Most Merciful. When the womb of his mother becomes too tight for him to remain in it (as he grows larger) Allaah guides the fetus to turn upside down in preparation to come out of the womb going through a tight passage, and he finds his way to it as if he was a grown up person who can reason and see his way out.

Once he comes out and needs food, He guides him to suckle his mother's nipple, and since his body is too little and cannot handle food, He decreed that pure milk comes out from between excretion and blood, and made the two nipples small enough to fit the mouth of the baby. He placed a hole in the nipple and made them tiny, which requires suckling before milk comes out and did not make it large lest the milk gushes out in large quantities because this small baby can only handle small quantities of milk.

Contemplate how Allaah guided the baby to the way of suckling in order to get the milk out when he is hungry.

Contemplate over the mercy and compassion of Allaah, how He delayed the growth of the teeth until the baby reaches the age of two because in the first two years he grows on milk and after that Allaah decrees for the teeth to grow because the baby would not be sufficed by the milk from his mother and requires food, which mandates that he has teeth to chew the food with; Allaah made the teeth grow when they are needed, not before and not after ... Glory be to Allaah, how He made hard bones grow out from the soft gum in the mouth!

Contemplate over the mercy Allaah placed in his parent's hearts to take care of his needs because he is incapable of taking care of his own affairs. Had Allaah not place such mercy in their hearts, the baby would have been so helpless!

Contemplate how Allaah gradually granted him the ability, the mind, and the guidance, and he grows to be a boy, then a teenager, then a young man, then a man, and then an old, helpless man. Through these stages, man is either grateful to Allaah or ungrateful, either obedient or disobedient, as Allaah Says (what means): *"Has there [not] period of time when he was not a thing [even] mentioned? Indeed, We created man from a sperm-drop mixture [i.e. a combination of the male and female substance, within the* *womb] that We may try him; and We made him hearing and seeing. Indeed, We guided him to the way, be he grateful or be he ungrateful."* [QUR'AAN 76:1-3]

After one contemplates his own creation, he should contemplate the earth in which he lives, and the rivers, the mountains and all the minerals it contains, then one should go higher and contemplate the vast heavens. Contemplate how Allaah turns the dry, dead, still earth into a productive one by sending down the rain and causing plants to quiver, grow and produce all types of plantations.

Contemplate how Allaah created the solid tough mountains and made them the cause for the earth to remain still. Look how He instilled water under these mountains and caused springs to gush with water, and made rivers flow on the surface of the earth, and brought about pure water from between rocks and mud, and made it (the pure water) the reason for the life of everything. Allaah made it the cause for different trees to grow, plants to yield fruits and vegetables; grapes, olives, palm trees, pomegranates and many other countless types of fruits, with different shapes, colors, taste and types. Allaah made some of these fruits exceed others in quality, though they are all watered with the same water and grow from one soil. One of the signs of Allaah are the gems He instilled under the mountains and the minerals.

There are no inanimate objects, animals or plants except that one would find that there is wisdom behind its creation. Allaah did not create anything aimlessly, in vain or in play. Rather, He created everything as it should be created in a manner that fits His majesty, generosity and compassion.

Another one of His signs are the different types of animals, birds and insects. Some of them walk, and others fly. Among those that walk are animals with two legs and others with four legs; and some of the insects walk on ten and other on a hundred.

One should remember the wonders of the spider, which is one of the small creatures. Contemplate its structure and house, and how it collects its food, how it treats the male, how it saves food, and how it designs its house. One sees a spider building a house on the bank of the river. It looks for two spots with a gap between them that is with the length of its arm or shorter in order to be able to connect the two sides with its thread. After that it starts discharging saliva to glue the thread with it, and then it goes to the opposite side and tightens the other side of the thread, and it keeps goings back and forth connecting threads while keeping the same distance between the threads. When it finishes tightening all threads on both sides, it starts connecting them together in an amazing engineering feat until it forms a net which catches flies and bugs. Then it sits in a corner waiting for something to fall in the net, and as soon as something falls in the net, it rushes to it and eats it. If it is unable to catch anything, it sits in a corner on a wall and connects the two sides of the angle of the wall by a thread and hangs itself on it using another thread, and then it remains still waiting for a fly to pass by it. As soon as a fly passes by it, it throws itself on it and traps the legs of the fly with the thread it was hanging with and starts eating it.

There is not an animal, small or big, except that it has countless wonders in it. Do you think (O son of Aadam) that the spider learnt these methods by itself? Do you think that the spider shaped itself by itself or did a human shape and form it? Do you think that it has no guide or one to teach it what and how to do things?

Would anyone with insight doubt that this creation (the spider) is weak and helpless? In fact, even a huge elephant whose apparent outwardly appearance reflects strength is helpless, so what would be the case with this small tiny creation (the spider)? Doesn't this creation, with its shape, movements, and the wonders in it, reflect the greatness and wisdom, ability, and knowledge of The Creator?

A person with insight sees in this weak helpless creation the greatness of the Creator, His majesty, His perfect ability, and His wisdom. This is on the scale of this tiny creation, how would the case then be with all other creations?

This is an endless list, because animals are countless, and they have different shapes and movements, but man forgets and overlooks these wonders because of getting used to it by seeing them often. Man becomes astonished when he sees a new animal, even if it was a worm, and the amazement of the creation of Allaah is renewed in his heart, and he would say: 'Subhaana Allaah' (Glory be to Allaah), what an amazing creation!'

Man is amazed at the creation of the different animals and overlooks the wonders that are instilled in him!" [1]

What can help one to contemplate?

Contemplating is an action of the heart, and one can attain it through different means, such as the following:

Seeking refuge in Allaah from Satan: Satan took a pledge upon himself to deviate and seduce humans and Jinn, and Allaah enabled him to have soldiers and followers who would help do so. They are very keen on preventing man from performing good deeds, especially the actions of the heart, of which contemplating is one of them.

Al-Karmaani, may Allaah have mercy on him, said: "One of the signs which indicate that Satan possesses the slave is when he busies him from contemplating the signs and favors of Allaah

---

1 Ihyaa' 'Uloom Ad-Deen (435-442/4).

and thanking Allaah for them, and busies him with managing the affairs of this worldly life and collecting more of it." [1]

Allaah The Almighty guided us to seek refuge from Satan before reciting the Qur'aan because contemplating over the verses of the Qur'aan is one of the most important fields of contemplation, and thus seeking refuge in Allaah from Satan before one starts to recite is a means to repel his whispers and expel him.

Ibn Katheer, may Allaah have mercy on him, said: "The reason for seeking refuge from Satan prior to starting the recitation of the Qur'aan is to avoid him (Satan) confusing one when reciting, making him forget what he is reciting, and preventing the person from contemplating the verses he is reciting." [2]

Shunning sins: Allaah The Exalted deprived those who transgress the limits, those who reject the signs and verses of Allaah and those who refuse to abide by and submit to the rules of Allaah. Allaah The Almighty Says (what means):

"I will turn away from My signs those who are arrogant upon the earth without right; and if they should see every sign, they will not believe in it. And if they see the way of consciousness [reason and integrity], they will not adopt it

1 Tafseer An-Nasfi (227/4).
2 Tafseer Ibn Katheer (773/2).

as a way; but if they see the way of error, they will adopt it as a way. That is because they have denied Our signs and they were heedless of them." [QUR'AAN 7:146] **Al-Hasan Al-Basri, may Allaah have mercy on him, said commenting on this verse:**

"This means, I will deprive them from contemplating over My signs and commands." [1]

One of the greatest sins which deprive a person from being able to contemplate the greatness of Allaah is listening to music. Ibn Al-Jawzi, may Allaah have mercy on him, said:

"Know that listening to music busies the heart and prevents it from contemplating over the greatness of Allaah The Exalted." [2]

Dear Muslim, be keen not to succumb to your desires in order to avoid being deprived of this virtue.

Visiting the graves: Visiting graves is one of the important acts which set the hearts contemplating. When the slave visits the graves, he contemplates with insight and he realizes that a hole such as this will eventually be his abode, and this would encourage him to perform more and more good deeds.

---

1 Ihyaa' 'Uloom Ad-Deen (424/4).
2 Talbees Iblees (274).

Mugheeth Al-Usood, may Allaah have mercy on him, said: "Visit the graves; they make you contemplate." [1]

The benefits of contemplation

Our righteous Salaf, may Allaah have mercy on them, were conscious of the great benefits of contemplation and its fruits, and thus they encouraged themselves and others to contemplate, and considered contemplation one of the noble and most important deeds.

Ibn 'Abbaas, may Allaah be pleased with him, said: "Contemplating for an hour is better than praying the optional night prayer." [1] **A similar statement was also said by Abu Ad-Dardaa', may Allaah be pleased with him.** [2] **Al-Hasan Al-Basri, may Allaah have mercy on him, also confirmed this.** [3]

Ibn 'Abbaas, may Allaah be pleased with him, said: "Praying two short Rak'ahs with contemplation is better than praying the entire night with one's heart heedless." [4]

Muhammad ibn Ka'b Al-Qurathi, may Allaah have mercy on him, said: "To pray the optional night prayer reciting Chapters

---

1 Ahwaal Al-Quboor (238).

Az-Zalzalah and Al-Qaari'ah and contemplate over them is dearer to me than reciting the entire Qur'aan rapidly." [5]

The following are some of the benefits obtained from contemplation:

Exerting more efforts :

Ibn Al-Qayyim, may Allaah have mercy on him, said: "Contemplation results in love for Allaah and an increase in a person's knowledge. When one contemplates over the Hereafter and its honor and continuity, and compares it to this temporary worldly life and its baseness, he would favor the Hereafter and shun this worldly life. The more one contemplates over the shortness of this life and its temporariness, the harder he would work and the more effort he would exert, and he would utilize his time to the optimum." [6]

Ibn 'Abbaas, may Allaah be pleased with him, said: "Contemplating over good deeds drives the person to perform them, and contemplating over evil drives one to shun them." [7]

---

1 Al-'Athamah (302/1) by Abu Ask-Shaykh.
2 Hilyat Al-Awliyaa' (209/1) and Shu'ab Al-Eemaan (118) and Ibn As-Saa'id ruled it as authentic.
3 Az-Zuhd (272) by Imaam Ahmad.
4 Az-Zuhd Az-Zuhd (228, 1147) by Ibn Al-Mubaarak.
5 Az-Zuhd Az-Zuhd (287) by Ibn Al-Mubaarak.
6 Al-Fawaa'id (198).
7 Ihyaa' 'Uloom Ad-Deen (425/4).

Qataadah, may Allaah have mercy on him, said: "If one contemplates over his own creation, he would realize that he was created in this shape with flexible joints connecting his bones only for the purpose of worshipping Allaah." [1]

Wahb, may Allaah have mercy on him, said: "Never did someone contemplate for a long time but that he understood (the objective of life), and never did someone understand but he would increase in knowledge, and never did someone increase in knowledge but he would act upon it." [2]

Fearing Allaah and realizing His greatness :

Bishr ibn Al-Haarith, may Allaah have mercy on him, said: "If people contemplate over the greatness of Allaah, they would never disobey Allaah." [3]

Haatim, may Allaah have mercy on him, said: "Mentioning Allaah frequently increases one's love for Allaah, and frequent contemplation increases one's fear (of Allaah)." [4]

Some scholars said: "Contemplation removes heedlessness and results in the fear (of Allaah)." [5]

---

1 Tafseer Ibn Katheer (297/4).
2 Al-'Athamah (56) by Abu Ask-Shaykh.
3 Hilyat Al-Awliyaa' (337/8).
4 Ihyaa' 'Uloom Ad-Deen (425/4).
5 Tafseer An-Nasfi (198/1).

Loving the Lord :

The slave's love for Allaah results when he contemplates His favors upon him, because the nature of people is that they love whoever treats them kindly. Therefore, when the slave contemplates the countless favors Allaah has bestowed upon him, the slave would love Allaah and be content with Him.

Increasing faith :

Among the means of increasing one's faith is to contemplate over the signs of Allaah, the universe, and man's creation. This is because contemplation confirms in the heart of the slave the ability, strength, might, and mercy of Allaah and that he is The Ever- Living, and The Sustainer.

Khaleefah Al-'Abdi, may Allaah have mercy on him, said: "If Allaah was to be worshipped only if He is seen, then no one would have worshipped Allaah. The believers contemplate over the advent of the night with its darkness that overwhelms the horizon, and then the advent of daylight which removes the darkness of the night; the clouds which are controlled between the heavens and earth; the stars; and the alternation of the winter and the summer. The believers continue to contemplate over what Allaah has created, until their hearts become certain and confirm His lordship." [1]

---

1 Ad-Durr Al-Manthoor (343/4).

Knowing one's reality and reforming it :

When one contemplates over himself, he will discover his faults and good qualities. Al-Fudhayl, may Allaah have mercy on him, said: "Contemplation is like a mirror which shows one his faults and good qualities." [1]

When one discovers his reality, he will strive to reform it and correct his faults and develop his good qualities. Sufyaan ibn 'Uyaynah, may Allaah have mercy on him, used to say: "Contemplation is like a light which you bring to your heart." He, may Allaah have mercy on him, also used to say: "Contemplation is the key to mercy; don't you see that when one contemplates, he repents?" [2]

The fruit of contemplation is an increase in knowledge, and with more knowledge comes a change over the heart that makes a person more conscious of his faults, and fearful of the consequences of negligence and deficiency as regards acts of worship. Thus one becomes careful to put more effort into acts of worship; so whenever the state of the heart changes (for the better), the actions of the limbs too change for the better, and one's state reforms and improves and his status becomes loftier.

---

1 Hilyat Al-Awliyaa' (109/8) and Al-'Athamah (13) by Abu Ask-Shaykh.
2 Hilyat Al-Awliyaa' (306/7).

Mugheeth ibn Asmaa', may Allaah have mercy on him, said: "A man from the nations before you used to perform all types of sins, and once he contemplated over his life and said: 'O Allaah, forgive me.' And he died in that state, and Allaah forgave him." [1]

Improving the status of the Muslim Nation :

If we want to improve the status of the Muslims, then we must contemplate over the current situation and try to discover the faults, and compare its state now and its state during the time of the early Salaf, may Allaah have mercy on them. Why were they able to control the world, while we fear that others (from the disbelievers) would attack us day and night?

The famous Muslim reformers throughout history must have contemplated the state of the Muslim Nation during their time, and discerned what it lacked, what its problems were and where the gaps to be filled were, after which they put in great effort into obtaining means of strength and improving and developing the state of the Muslims, and filling in any open gaps.

Increasing one's knowledge :

Contemplation is a reason for which Allaah grants the slave knowledge and wisdom, and a means to understand Islamic legislation in the best manner and most perfect way.

---

1 Ad-Durr Al-Manthoor (58/4).

Abu Ad-Dardaa', may Allaah be pleased with him, said Luqmaan, may Allaah have mercy on him: "He did not obtain the status he did because of his family, wealth, lineage, or character; rather he was a man who was always silently contemplating for long hours with deep insight. He used to visit the rulers in order to contemplate over their situation and take lessons." [1]

Al-Hasan, may Allaah have mercy on him, said: "Sound-minded people continued to contemplate until their hearts opened up and they spoke words of wisdom." [2]

Abu Sulaymaan Ad-Daaraani, may Allaah have mercy on him, said: "Contemplation over (the pleasures of) this worldly life prevents one from contemplating over the Hereafter, which is a punishment; while contemplating over the Hereafter bestows the person wisdom and revives the heart." [3]

Ash-Shaafi'i, may Allaah have mercy on him, said: "If you want to utter wise words, then be silent more often (in order to weigh what you want to say before saying it) and if you want to reach correct deductions (in Islamic rules) contemplate for longer periods." [4] **He, may Allaah have mercy on him, also said:**

---

1 Tafseer Ibn Katheer (585/3).
2 Hilyat Al-Awliyaa' (19/10).
3 Ihyaa' 'Uloom Ad-Deen (425/4).
4 Miftaah As-Sa'aadah (180/1) and Faydh Al-Qadeer (314/2).

"Virtuous traits are four: First: wisdom which can be achieved by contemplation. Second: chastity which can be achieved by overcoming lusts. Third: strength which can be achieved by overcoming anger. Fourth: justice which can be achieved by balancing one's temper." [1]

How were the scholars able to produce this rich harvest of knowledge? How did they author all these books? How were they able to deduce all these rulings in the different sciences of Islamic knowledge?

Undoubtedly, a great portion of this was due to their contemplation over the signs of Allaah and His verses, and over events which took place before.

Solving difficult issues :

Abu Haneefah, may Allaah have mercy on him, was asked about two brothers who married two sisters, and they entered upon each other's wives by mistake (i.e. each of them entered the room of the other) and each one of them had intercourse with his brother's wife, and they only discovered this in the morning, what would the ruling be. He, may Allaah have mercy on him, contemplated for a long time and then came to the following result, he said: "O so and so, do you like the woman you slept with last night and are you content with her?" the man said: "Yes." Then he asked the other man: "O so and so, do you like the woman you slept with last night and are you content with

1 Ihyaa' 'Uloom Ad-Deen (425/4).

her?" the man said: "Yes." Thereupon he, may Allaah have mercy on him, said: "Each of you should divorce his actual wife and then each of you should marry the one he slept with." Then he concluded the marriage contract for each of them.

Being able to reconcile texts which appear to be contradictory:

Allaah The Almighty Says (what means): *"And no bearer of burdens will bear the burden of another."* [QUR'AAN 17:15]
The Prophet, sallallaahu 'alayhi wa sallam, said: *"The dead [person] is punished as a result of the weeping of his family over him."* [1]

The verse confirms that man will not shoulder the sin of others, while the narration confirms the dead person will be punished if his family wept over him. This case appears to be two contradicting texts, however, the scholars contemplated the texts and reached the conclusion that the punishment of the dead happens if he was the one commanding his family to weep aloud over his death, which means that the punishment resulted due to his own action.

---

1 Reported by Al-Bukhaari (1242) and Muslim (927).

Combining between worship and contemplation

'Abdullaah ibn 'Abbaas, may Allaah be pleased with him, narrated that he spent one night at the house of Maymoonah, may Allaah be pleased with her, (his maternal aunt and the wife of the Prophet of Allaah, sallallaahu 'alayhi wa sallam). He, sallallaahu 'alayhi wa sallam, slept until it was midnight or shortly before or after that, then he woke up and wiped the trace of sleep from his face with his hands, and then recited the last ten verses of Chapter Aal 'Imraan, and then he, sallallaahu 'alayhi wa sallam, stood up to pray. [1]

As soon as he, sallallaahu 'alayhi wa sallam, woke up, he would start to contemplate over the last ten verses of Chapter Aal 'Imraan which he was commanded to contemplate over. This is the way a Muslim should be: combine between worship and contemplation. One should not spend all his time contemplating without performing acts of worship, nor should he spend all his time worshipping without contemplating; rather, one should combine between the two.

Ibn Al-'Arabi, may Allaah have mercy on him, comments on the action of the Prophet, sallallaahu 'alayhi wa sallam, saying: "Look how he combined between contemplating over the creation, and then hastening to pray just after that. This is the

1 Reported by Al-Bukhaari (183) and Muslim (763).

way people should adopt. As for the way of the Soofis whose Shaykh (or leader) stays in contemplation for a day and a night, and sometimes for a full month without stopping; this is incorrect and is not suitable for humans, and it does not agree with the Sunnah." [1]

A Muslim should combine between the two actions and should not pay attention to one and neglect the other because this could lead him to error.

Our Salaf and contemplation

A Muslim should follow in the footsteps of the righteous Salaf from the Companions, may Allaah be pleased with them, and the generation who came after them and those who followed into their footsteps until the Day of Resurrection.

Our Salaf were aware of the importance of contemplation, and thus they performed it a lot, acted upon it and made it part of their daily life.

Muhammad ibn Waasi', may Allaah have mercy on him, narrated that a man from the people of Basra (in Iraq) travelled to see Umm Tharr, may Allaah be pleased with her, after the death of Abu Tharr, may Allaah be pleased with him, in order to ask her about his way of worship. He asked her saying: "I came

1 Tafseer Al-Qurtubi (301/4).

to ask you about the worship of Abu Tharr." She said: "He used to spend his days in contemplation." [1]

'Awn, may Allaah have mercy on him, said: "We asked Umm Ad-Dardaa' about the best act of worship used to perform. She replied: 'Contemplation and taking lessons.'" [2]

'Abdullaah ibn Al-Mubaarak, may Allaah have mercy on him, said one day to Sahl ibn 'Adiyy, may Allaah have mercy on him, when he saw him silent and thinking: "Where have you reached (with your contemplation)?" he replied: "The Siraat (over the fire of Hell)" [3]

'Umar ibn 'Abdul-'Azeez, may Allaah have mercy on him, cried one day while he was sitting with his companions, and when they asked him about the reason for his crying he replied: "I contemplated over this worldly life and its pleasures and desires and took lessons from it. As soon as one fulfills the desires it has, it (the joy of the desire) is ruined by the bitterness of its (evil) consequence. If there are no lessons in it for those who ponder, it certainly has admonishments for those who contemplate." [4]

---

1 Hilyat Al-Awliyaa' (164/1).
2 Hilyat Al-Awliyaa' (300/7).
3 Ihyaa' 'Uloom Ad-Deen (425/4).
4 Tafseer Ibn Katheer (439/1).

Once Sufyaan Ath-Thawri, may Allaah have mercy on him, was sitting in a gathering, and suddenly the lamp went off and darkness covered the room. When the lamp was lit again, people found Sufyaan broke into profuse tears, so they asked him: "What is wrong with you?" he replied: "I remembered the (darkness of the) grave."

People said to Ibraaheem, may Allaah have mercy on him: "Why do you contemplate for a long time?" He answered: "Contemplation is the energizer of the brain." [1]

Abu Shurayh, may Allaah have mercy on him, was walking one day, and suddenly he sat down and veiled his face and started to cry. People asked him about the reason he was crying, so he said: "I contemplated over my life and how it passed, and how little my deeds are, and how near my death is." [2]

Daawood At-Taa'i, may Allaah have mercy on him, was contemplating during a full-moon night, and then he stood up and went up to the roof and started to walk while looking in the horizon, so he fell to his next door neighbor's house. The house owner rushed out, and took his sword thinking it was a thief. When he saw that it was Daawood, he went back and returned his sword, and then took Daawood by his hand and walked him to his house. When Daawood was asked about what had

1 Miftaah Daar As-Sa'aadah (180/1).
2 Reported by Ibn Abu Shaybah in his book Al-'Umur Wash-Shayb (22).

happened he said: "I was contemplating and did not feel what happened." [1]

Haatim, may Allaah have mercy on him, said: "Whoever passes by the graveyard and does not contemplate over his situation, and supplicate for the dead has betrayed himself and betrayed them." [2]

One of the devout worshippers took a mug of water to perform ablution before praying the optional night prayer. When he entered his finger in the narrow part of the mug he started contemplating until it was time to pray Fajr. When he was asked about this, he said: "I remembered the saying of Allaah The Exalted (which means): *"When the shackles are around their necks and the chains"* [QUR'AAN 40:71] **and started to think how would I be if these shackles were to be thrown on me, and I stayed all night contemplating over this."** [3]

One of the Salaf passed by a baker who was baking some bread, and started to look at the fire, and then broke into tears and cried very hard. When people asked him about the reason for his crying, he said: "I remembered the fire of Hell."

---

1 Hilyat Al-Awliyaa' (280/8).
2 Al-'Aaqibah Fi Thikr Al-Mawt(195).
3 Tafseer Al-Qurtubi (245/8).

This is how the righteous Salaf, may Allaah have mercy on them, were and this was their contemplation, so will we take them as examples and follow in their footsteps?

Conclusion

The heart which does not contemplate over the creation of Allaah and His signs is a dead heart. Beneficial contemplation is that which one does with insight and aims at taking lessons. As for those who contemplate just to gain more knowledge and do not aim at acting upon the knowledge they gain from contemplation, then such a person is one who wrongs himself.

A person should contemplate a lot, because it leads to the pleasure of Allaah, comforts the heart and brings tranquility to it, and results in fearing Allaah and makes the person gain wisdom, knowledge and insight and revives his heart.

Remember your destiny and the place you are heading towards; contemplate over the portion of your life which has already passed: do you trust that what you did in it will grant you salvation and save you from the punishment of your Lord? Or will you find sins and evil deeds and shortcomings which will lead you to destruction? Beware of feeling secure while leading

a heedless life, the life of those whose main concern is to follow their desires and fulfill them.

We ask Allaah to make us among those who contemplate, think and take lessons.

Test your understanding

Here are two levels of questions about the topic; there are direct questions, meaning, the first level questions, and questions that need some research and reflection, which are the second level questions.

Level one questions:

1. **State the definition of Taahir 'Aashoor, may Allaah have mercy on him, for contemplation?**
2. **What is the ruling of contemplation? What is the evidence for this?**
3. **List the four fields of contemplation.**
4. **What are the things which can help one contemplate?**
5. **What are the fruits and benefits of contemplation?**
6. **Give examples of contemplation done by our Salaf?**
7. **Why did Allaah enumerate for His slaves the types of creation that exist in the heavens and earth?**

Level two questions:

1. **What are the boundaries of praised contemplation and how can one govern it?**

2. **Explain the following statement: "He who knows his reality will know his Lord".**
3. **How can contemplation help increase the level of faith?**
4. **Is there a connection between worship and contemplation?**
5. **What are things that can help a person contemplate (other than what was mentioned above)?**

CPSIA information can be obtained
at www.ICGtesting.com
Printed in the USA
LVHW021953150722
723616LV00017B/1232

9 784869 909360